I0782045

Identify 25 Beautiful Birds &
Become a Backyard Birder! - A Fun
Guide with Pictures, Descriptions,
Tips & Interesting Facts

B.M. Gonzales Authors

I am delighted that you have picked this guide to accompany you on your South Texas birding expedition! As a long-time birder who has spent many hours searching the undergrowth and listening to the symphony of sounds in our unique habitat, I can assure you that there is nothing quite like it.

You may be wondering why a full handbook is devoted to birdwatching in South Texas. Okay, let me tell you a tale. A few years ago, a newcomer with a blossoming interest in birds arrived in my neighborhood. They were anxious to learn but were overwhelmed by the sheer quantity of feathery buddies flying about. There were just too many options, and too many strange names and faces.

That is where the seed for this guide was planted. I wanted to build a resource that would bridge that gap, providing a welcoming introduction to the diverse world of South Texas birds.

This book is intended to function as both binoculars and a birdwatching diary, assisting you in identifying frequent backyard visits, understanding their intriguing routines, and quickly becoming a competent birder.

Consider it a compass; it will guide you across varied ecosystems, from quiet waterways to lively grasslands, leading you to the most beautiful avian occupants. We'll look at the obstacles of drawing these feathered beauties to your yard but don't worry, we'll also provide answers,

Happy Birding!

Contents

Why Birdwatch in South Texas?

South Texas, an area of natural miracles, invites birdwatchers with an avian richness unlike any other in the United States. A patchwork of habitats unfolds here, at the junction of multiple biomes - the Tamaulipan thorn scrub, the Chihuahuan Desert, the enormous Gulf Coast plain, and the life-giving ribbon of the Rio Grande - each with its own unique and intriguing assembly of feathered occupants.

This amazing natural patchwork results in a stunning abundance of birds. Over 530 species have been reported in South Texas, demonstrating the region's unique position as a vital crossroads for migrating birds and a year-round shelter for resident wildlife. From the showy Altamira Oriole, a flash of brightness amongst the prickly scrub, to the secretive Plain Chachalaca, whose throaty notes resonate through the deep forests, South Texas has a dazzling assortment of bird encounters.

- **Tamaulipan Thorn Scrub:** This dry habitat, characterized by drought-resistant acacias and cacti, is home to a variety of specialized birds. Look for the curvy Curve-billed Thrasher, with its long, sharply curved beak ideal for removing insects from thorny foliage. The beautiful song of the Buff-throated Woodpecker, a cavity nester that prefers these dry forests, is another treat for the birding ear.

- **Chihuahuan Desert:** Explore the parched stretches of the Chihuahuan Desert and meet a diverse cast of avian species. The acrobatic Scissor-tailed Flycatcher, with its captivating scissor-like tail, conducts aerial ballets to capture flying insects. The appropriately called Greater Roadrunner, a long-legged, ground-dwelling bird, races over the desert floor in a flurry of brown, leaving smaller prey behind.

- **Gulf Coast Plain: As** you approach the dazzling Gulf Coast, the terrain changes into a tapestry of marshes, barrier islands, and coastal plains. Graceful wading birds such as the Great Blue

Heron and Green Heron patrol the shallows, while the spectacular White-winged Dove, with its characteristic whistle, may be seen in broad fields and scattered trees. Don't miss the opportunity to see the spectacular Anhinga, a long-necked, snake-like waterbird that deftly dives underwater in search of fish.

- **Rio Grande Valley:** The Rio Grande River, South Texas' lifeblood, creates a beautiful green corridor across the parched country. This riparian ribbon offers critical habitat for a diverse range of bird species. The Altamira Oriole, a jewel-toned dweller of the valley's forests, has a vivid song that is enchanting. Keep an eye out for the vividly colored Northern Flicker, a woodpecker that feeds on both trees and the ground, and listen for the rattling cry of the elusive Least Grebe, a small diving bird located in quiet coves.

Diverse Birdlife

South Texas is a sanctuary for both local and migratory birds. Over 150 species breed here, taking advantage of the area's warm winters and plentiful food supplies.

These permanent populations are supplemented by a remarkable number of migratory birds, with certain species making South Texas a key stopover on their lengthy treks between North and South America. This flow of migrants adds a dynamic aspect to the birding experience, providing opportunities to see a diverse range of feathered visitors throughout the year.

Year-round Birding:

Unlike many other places, where birding activity diminishes during the cold winter months, South Texas allows you to enjoy birdwatching all year. The warm winters attract overwintering species such as the vividly colorful Northern Cardinal and the lively Carolina Chickadee, while the spring and summer see an explosion in breeding activity, with both resident and migratory birds rearing their young. Fall brings another influx of avian guests as migrating birds make their journey south for the winter, providing a rare chance to experience the fascinating phenomena of bird migration firsthand.

What You'll Find in This Guide

This thorough book is intended to be an important companion on your South Texas birding journey. Whether you're an experienced birder or just getting started, this resource will provide you with the information and resources you need to recognize birds, understand their behavior, and create a bird-friendly refuge in your backyard.

The following chapters go deep into the world of South Texas birds, offering specific information on:

- Learn how to recognize birds by sight and sound, traverse varied environments, and make the most use of field guides and birding apps.

- Common backyard visits are the cherry House Finch and the melodious Mockingbird. We'll provide you with extensive descriptions, habitat preferences, and intriguing information about each species so you can become a backyard birding expert.

- South Texas' avian highlights include the elusive Plain Chachalaca and the bright Altamira Oriole. We'll look at their intriguing adaptations, preferred habitats, and advice for identifying these unique inhabitants.

- **Birding hotspots:** Get out of your neighborhood and discover the region's top birding areas, from state parks and wildlife refuges to secret birding paths. We'll give extensive descriptions, and access information, and emphasize the distinct birdlife that each place has.

- **Creating a bird-friendly backyard:** Make your backyard a paradise for feathered guests. Learn about the significance of native flora, food, and water supplies, and appropriate shelter locations. We'll provide you with practical methods and guidance for attracting a wide variety of birds to your yard.

- **Birding throughout the year:** Learn how the seasons affect bird behavior in South Texas. We'll talk about migratory patterns, nesting habits, and the ideal times of year to watch certain bird species.
- **Keeping a Bird watching journal:** You may become a citizen scientist by recording your birding experiences. Learn how to document your encounters, follow bird activity, and give essential information to the protection of these amazing species.

This book is more than simply a list of facts and data; it's an invitation to discover the delights of South Texas' avian world. With in-depth knowledge, practical recommendations, and a dash of local birding history, this resource will help you become a confident and enthusiastic birder, ready to discover the secrets of the feathered gems that decorate this magnificent area.

Getting Started With Backyard Birding

Welcome to your birding refuge, your backyard! Transforming this place into a refuge for feathered companions is not only gratifying, but it also contributes significantly to local bird populations. This chapter digs into the fundamentals of establishing a bird-friendly backyard, attracting a varied range of feathered guests, and seeing nature's marvels develop right outside your window.

Creating a Bird-Friendly Backyard

Native Plants:

The careful use of native plants is essential to creating a successful bird-friendly refuge. These Indigenous species provide a variety of advantages for birds:

- **Food supply:** Native plants have developed with local bird species, giving a consistent and healthy food supply. Native plant fruits, berries, and seeds are ideally matched to unique avian diets. For example, hungry Northern Cardinals like the vivid orange berries of Firebush (Hamelia patens), while hummingbirds seek the nectar-rich blossoms of Coral Honeysuckle (Lonicera sempervirens) for a refreshing energy boost.

- **Insect Buffets:** Many natural plants maintain a wide population of insects, which provide an important food source for insectivorous birds. Caterpillars and other invertebrates thrive among oaks (Quercus spp.), while natural grasses such as Little Bluestem (Schizachyrium scoparium) offer a home for beetles and grasshoppers, both of which are easily ingested by foraging birds such as Carolina Chickadees and Eastern Meadowlarks.

- **Protection and Nesting Sites:** Native trees and bushes provide vital protection for birds, shielding them from predators and severe weather. Native plants like Buttonbush (Cephalanthus occidentalis) develop dense thickets that offer

nesting places for a variety of songbirds, whilst cavity-nesting birds like woodpeckers benefit from old trees with naturally existing holes or holes made by intentional pruning.

Food and Water Sources:

Aside from native plants, providing extra food and water sources in your garden would greatly increase its attraction to birds.

- **Food:** Offer a range of food alternatives to accommodate various bird species. Cardinals, finches, and chickadees are attracted to platform feeders with black oil sunflower seeds. Suet feeders provide a high-energy meal for insect-eating birds such as woodpeckers and nuthatches. Hummingbird feeders packed with a sugar-water mix serve as a key energy source for these aerial acrobats. Ground feeders with millet and cracked corn attract sparrows, doves, and other ground-feeding birds. Remember to replace feeders regularly and carefully clean them to minimize illness transmission.

- **Water:** A consistent supply of fresh water is critical for birds, particularly during hot and dry spells. A small birdbath set on a sturdy platform allows birds to drink and wash. Moving water, delivered by a solar-powered fountain or a dripper attachment, is even more appealing to certain bird species. To avoid mosquito breeding, keep the birdbath clean and refresh the water regularly.

Shelter:

Providing a range of shelter alternatives ensures that your backyard meets the different requirements of birds. Dense evergreen bushes such as Eastern Red Cedar (Juniperus virginiana) provide year-round shelter, and brush piles made from fallen branches provide a secure sanctuary for ground-dwelling birds. Climbing vines, such as Virginia Creeper (Parthenocissus quinquefolia), offer birds more perching and nesting opportunities.

Additional Considerations:

- **Minimize Grass Area:** Birds find little food or refuge in large areas of grass. Consider transforming a piece of your lawn into a native plant garden or a wildflower meadow to create a more natural and bird-friendly habitat.

- **Reduce Pesticide Use:** Pesticides not only kill important insects that birds consume, but they may also be hazardous to birds themselves. Choose natural pest control solutions wherever feasible.

- **Let Some Things Go:** A little controlled anarchy might be useful. Leaving fallen leaves and dead branches in your yard offers insects refuge while also creating natural feeding opportunities for birds.

By adding these features, you'll be well on your way to building a vibrant backyard environment that not only attracts birds but also sustains a diverse range of species.

Attracting Birds With Feeders

Types of Feeders:

The sort of feeder you use depends on the particular birds you want to attract.

- **Platform Feeders:** These adaptable feeders provide a broad range of feeding alternatives, including black oil sunflower seeds and mealworms. They attract a wide variety of birds, such as cardinals, chickadees, finches, and grackles.

- **Tube Feeders:** These feeders have several feeding openings and are great for dispersing tiny seeds such as thistle and nyjer. They typically attract finches, goldfinches, and redpolls.

- **Suet Feeders:** Suet feeders, which are usually cages filled with suet cake, attract insect-eating birds such as woodpeckers, nuthatches, and wrens. Suet is a high-energy food source, particularly in the winter months when natural insect prey is limited.

- **Hopper Feeders:** These feeders, which have a hopper that distributes seed as birds eat, are an excellent choice for attracting ground-feeding birds such as sparrows, doves, and juncos. Scattering seeds on the ground near the feeder might also draw these birds.

- **Hummingbird Feeders:** These specialty feeders, with red reservoirs, distribute a sugar-water mix to attract hummingbirds. Different feeder designs appeal to particular hummingbird species, so choose a feeder based on the local hummingbird population.

Choosing The Right Seeds:

The sort of seed you give will have a big influence on the birds you attract.

- **Black Oil Sunflower Seeds:** These high-energy seeds are popular with birds such as cardinals, chickadees, finches, and grackles. To avoid the hassle of discarded shells, use hulled sunflower seeds instead.
- **Nyjer Seed:** These small, oil-rich seeds attract finches, especially goldfinches and redpolls.
- **Thistle:** Like nyjer seed, thistle attracts a variety of finches.
- **Millet**: This little, white seed is popular with ground-feeding birds like sparrows and doves.
- **Cracked Corn:** Larger birds, such as jays and crows, like a dish of cracked corn placed on the ground.
- **Suet cakes** come in a variety of tastes, such as plain suet, peanut butter suet, and bug suet. Choose a taste depending on the birds you want to attract.
- **Sugar-Water Solution:** For hummingbirds, mix 1:4 sugar to water. Boil the water first to thoroughly dissolve the sugar, then let it cool before filling the feeder. Never use honey or artificial sweeteners in hummingbird feeders.

Place feeders in a covered place, away from windows, to avoid bird collisions. Ideally, position feeders near trees or bushes where birds feel secure and can flee quickly if a predator appears.

- **Multiple Feeders:** Providing a variety of feeders with varying seed varieties helps attract a broader assortment of birds.

- **Cleanliness Matters**: To avoid illness transmission among birds, clean your feeders regularly using a mild soap solution.

- **Be patient:** Birds may take some time to find your feeders. Be patient and persistent in your efforts, and you'll soon be rewarded with a flock of feathery guests.

By applying these ideas, you can turn your backyard into a bird refuge, providing them with a consistent food supply, freshwater, and necessary shelter. Witnessing these beautiful species darting about and enjoying your backyard refuge will be a rewarding experience for you as well as a useful addition to your local environment.

Birdwatching Essentials

Equipping oneself with the proper equipment can greatly improve your birding experience in South Texas. Here's a rundown of the most important things for every aspiring birder:

Binoculars:

Binoculars provide you access to a world of avian detail. Consider the following variables when selecting the ideal pair for South Texas birding:

- **Magnification**: For birding in South Texas, an 8x to 10x magnification is recommended. Higher magnification provides a closer picture but might be difficult to maintain steady.
- The objective lens diameter controls how much light enters the binoculars, which affects visual brightness and clarity. A bigger objective lens (e.g., 42mm) is very useful in low-light situations like early mornings and nights.
- **Field of View:** This is the area you can see via the binoculars at a particular distance. A broader range of vision makes it easier to detect birds, particularly amid thick foliage.

- Eye Relief is the distance between your eye and the eyepiece that allows you to view a clear picture. If you use spectacles, buy binoculars with enough eye relief to provide a pleasant vision.
- **Waterproof and fog-proof:** The weather in South Texas is unpredictable. Choose binoculars that are both waterproof and fogproof to guarantee excellent performance in all situations.

Field Guides:

A good field guide is a helpful tool for identifying birds. When picking a field guide for South Texas, consider the following points:

- **Regional Focus:** Select a field guide prepared exclusively for the birds of South Texas. This guarantees that the book includes information on the most common resident and migratory species.
- **Organization:** Some field guides are divided into bird families, while others utilize a color-coded scheme. Choose a format that fits your learning approach and helps you to rapidly find bird descriptions.
- **Images:** High-quality images that depict plumage variances (breeding vs. non-breeding), age

differences, and distinguishing markings are essential for proper identification.

- **Species Descriptions:** Detailed species descriptions should contain information about size, coloring, sounds, and habitat preferences. Look for a handbook that has short and helpful text to match the pictures.

Apps:

Birding applications provide an abundance of information and capabilities at your fingertips. Here are some characteristics to consider.

- **Bird Identification Tools:** Many birding apps include AI-powered picture recognition or bird call identification tools to assist you in identifying unfamiliar species.

- **Species Information:** Birding apps, like field guides, contain thorough information about bird species, such as descriptions, calls, and distribution maps.

- **Field Observations:** Some applications let you see real-time sightings recorded by other birders in your vicinity. This might be useful for spotting certain bird species or finding new birding sites.

- **The bird cries and Songs:** Understanding bird cries is an important ability for birders. Apps may give recordings of bird cries and songs, enabling you to practice identifying birds by ear.

While not required, a notepad and a tiny pen are useful for documenting your sightings, including the date, location, bird species, and any notable remarks. A compact camera with a decent zoom lens may also be beneficial for photographing birds, particularly for future identification or reference.

Safety Considerations.

While bringing birds to your backyard is a good thing, you should be aware of possible safety concerns:

Unwanted Animal Visitors:
Bird feeders might attract unexpected animals:

- **Squirrels:** These acrobatic rodents often make frequent visits to bird feeders. Squirrel baffles installed around feeder poles may prevent squirrels from obtaining the seed. Alternatively, give squirrel-specific feeders packed with nuts or maize to deflect their interest.

- **Raccoons** are nocturnal creatures that may plunder feeders at night. To prevent raccoons, strategically place feeders away from trees or buildings that they may readily climb. Metal feeders with lockable lids may also serve as effective deterrents.

- **Predatory Birds:** While bringing hawks and owls to your yard might be thrilling, these birds of prey may also endanger smaller songbirds that use your feeders. Providing sufficient cover around feeders, such as thick bushes or small trees, helps songbirds flee quickly if a predator comes.

<u>**Window Collisions:**</u>

Birds may crash with glass, mistaking their reflection for vast space. Here are some techniques to lessen the risk:

- Place Feeders at least three feet away from windows to reduce the possibility of birds mistaking the reflection for a feeding location.
- **Use Window Decals:** Applying decals or patterned film to your windows will help birds see the glass and avoid mistaking it for open space. For the best results, use vertical stripes that are tightly spaced (no more than two inches apart). Etching or icing the bottom half of your glass may provide a similar effect.
- **Keep Your Blinds Closed:** Closing blinds or curtains on bright days might help to lessen the reflecting characteristics of your windows.

By taking these precautions, you may enjoy attracting birds to your backyard while reducing the chance of interactions with nuisance creatures and window crashes. Remember that a little foresight and preventive effort may go a long way toward providing a safe and stimulating habitat for both birds and people.

Introduction to Bird Identification.

Welcome to the thriving world of South Texas birds. Before we get into the particular feathered inhabitants you'll see in your backyard and beyond, let's start with a basic understanding of bird anatomy and the main bird kinds prevalent in this area.

Bird Anatomy: A Birdwatcher's Toolkit

Understanding a bird's fundamental anatomy is critical for proper identification. Here's a summary of the essential characteristics to focus on:

- **Bill**: The bill, also known as the beak, varies in form and size depending on the bird's food and eating habits. A broad, robust bill is suggestive of a seed-eating bird, such as a cardinal, but a long, thin beak is appropriate for probing insects, such as the Carolina Chickadee.

- Check for the presence or absence of crests, wattles, or facial marks. These characteristics may be unique and important for identification.

- **Eye color** may vary greatly, which can aid in distinguishing between similar-looking species. Pay attention to eye location as well; birds with eyes on the sides of their heads, such as owls, have a larger field of vision for hunting prey, but birds with eyes closer to the front of the head, such as chickadees, have superior depth perception.

- **The length and thickness of the neck** may provide useful information. Long necks distinguish wading birds such as herons and egrets, enabling them to feed in deeper water.

- **Body Size and Shape:** Birds come in a wide variety of sizes, from the tiny hummingbird to the stately turkey vulture. Overall body shape may also be diagnostic; for example, woodpeckers have a stocky physique with powerful legs to cling to tree trunks, while swallows have a streamlined body and long, pointed wings to perform agile aerial acrobatics.

- **Wing form and size** are strongly related to a bird's flying style and habitat choice. Soaring birds, such as hawks and eagles, have broad, rounded wings, but swallows and falcons have long, pointed wings.

- **The length, form, and pigment of the tail** may be important identifying markers. Some birds, such as the Scissor-tailed Flycatcher, have very long, forked tails, but others, such as woodpeckers, rely on their stiff tail feathers for support when climbing trees.

- **Legs and Feet:** The length and form of a bird's legs and feet provide details about its feeding style. Long legs distinguish wading birds, but raptors have formidable talons for capturing prey. Perching birds have three toes in the front and one in the rear, which enable them to grab trees tightly. Waterfowl have webbed feet so they can swim.

- **Plumage (feathers)** is the most visually prominent element and plays an important part in bird identification. Examine the general color patterns, markings, and any distinctions between males and females (sexual differentiation).

By meticulously evaluating these anatomical traits, you'll have a sharp eye for recognizing South Texas' various avian inhabitants.

Common Bird Types of South Texas

South Texas has a tremendous diversity of bird life, including both permanent and migratory species. Here's a look at some of the most frequent bird varieties you'll encounter:

- **Songbirds,** often known as passerines, are the most common and diversified kind of bird in South Texas. They include common garden birds such as cardinals, chickadees, finches, and mockingbirds. Songbirds have a diverse range of vocalizations and are generally brilliantly colored, especially during the mating season.
- **Wading Birds:** These long-legged birds, with their long necks and beaks, are ideal for foraging in shallow water. Herons, egrets, and ibises are often seen in wetlands, marshes, and along the Rio Grande River.

- **Waterfowl** include ducks, geese, and swans, who are excellent swimmers and divers. Several species of waterfowl travel through South Texas, making use of the area's valuable wetlands and coastal habitats.

- **Raptors:** Birds of prey such as hawks, owls, falcons, and vultures play an important role in the ecology by limiting the numbers of small mammals and reptiles. Raptors use excellent vision, strong talons, and hooked beaks to hunt.

- **Shorebirds** are migratory birds with long legs and narrow beaks that inhabit mudflats, beaches, and coastal environments. Sandpipers, plovers, and turnstones are some of the shorebirds that may be seen in South Texas, particularly during their spring and autumn migrations.

- **Ground Birds:** These birds spend a large amount of time on the ground, hunting for grains and insects. Ground birds found in South Texas include quails, doves, and roadrunners. These birds' plumage is generally cryptic, allowing them to blend in with their surroundings.

- **Woodpeckers** are readily identified by their powerful bills and tapping noises. Woodpeckers use their beak to create nesting chambers in trees and retrieve insects from under the bark. Several woodpecker species, notably the Golden-fronted and Ladder-backed Woodpecker, are prevalent in South Texas forests.

- **Hummingbirds** are small, jewel-like birds with amazing flying abilities. They hover above blooms while consuming nectar, using their extended bills and quick wing beats. South Texas is home to various hummingbird species, including the colorful Ruby-throated Hummingbird and the somewhat bigger Buff-bellied Hummingbird.

This is just a quick introduction to South Texas' rich avian life. As you go on your birding travels, you'll come across a diverse range of feathered inhabitants, each with its own adaptations and intriguing activities. The next chapters will go further into various bird groups and species, including thorough descriptions, habitat preferences, and identification hints to help you become a confident and informed birder in this beautiful area.

Meet Your Feathered Friends—25 Easy-to-Identify Birds of South Texas.

Welcome back, birding enthusiast! Now that you've learned the principles of bird identification and are familiar with the most frequent bird varieties in South Texas, let's meet some of the feathered inhabitants you're likely to see in your backyard!

Backyard Visitors:

1. The Northern Cardinal (Cardinalis cardinalis)

- **Description:** This distinctive songbird is a brilliant shade of red. Males have a brilliant red body, a black mask, and a pointed conical bill. Females are more muted brownish-red, with minor striping over the breast. Both sexes wear a

conspicuous crest on their heads.

- **Habitat:**  Northern Cardinals flourish in a wide range of settings, including backyards, gardens, forests, and shrublands. They easily adapt to bird feeders and are common in cities and suburbs.

- **Interesting Fact:** Throughout the year, the male Cardinal sings a complicated song to protect his territory and attract mates. Females also sing, although their songs are simpler and shorter than males'.

- **Tips for Identification:** The male Northern Cardinal's striking red plumage is easily identifiable. Look for a black mask with a crest on the head. Females may be mistaken with other brown birds, but their general reddish color and lack of noticeable markings distinguish them.

2.   Mourning Dove (Zenaida macroura)

Description: This lovely dove is a frequent garden visitor. Adults are light grayish brown, with a long, pointed tail and a tiny head. They have a conspicuous black patch on each cheek and a white border along the trailing edge of their wings.

- **Habitat:** Mourning Doves live in a range of open environments, such as fields, meadows, backyards, and parks. They can easily adapt to urban and suburban surroundings.

- **Interesting Fact:** Mourning Doves communicate with one another using a melancholy cooing sound known as "who-cooks-for-you."

- **Tips for Identification:** The Mourning Dove is distinguished by its grayish-brown hue, long tail, and black cheek mark. Listen for their melancholy cooing cry to assist identification.

3. House Finch (Haemorhous mexicanus)

Description: This energetic songbird often visits backyards and bird feeders. Males have bright red breasts, striped brown backs, and white bellies. Females resemble sparrows in appearance, with streaked brown plumage and slight wing bars.

Habitat: House Finches flourish in a wide range of settings, including backyards, gardens, forests, and shrublands. They easily adapt to urban and suburban environments and are drawn to bird feeders.

Interesting fact: Male House Finches get their red hue from their eating. They receive carotenoids from the seeds they consume and deposit them in their feathers.

Tips for Identification: The male House Finch's red breast is an obvious indicator. Female sparrows might be more difficult to identify, but their streaked brown plumage and lack of noticeable markings make them stand out from the others.

4.   Carolina   Chickadee   (Poecile carolinensis).

• **Description:** This little, active songbird is a welcome addition to backyards and forests. Adults are grayish-brown overall, with a black head and bib that contrast with white cheeks. They have a small, pointed beak and a lengthy tail.

Habitat: Carolina Chickadees inhabit deciduous woods, woodlands, and well-vegetated backyards. They often visit bird feeders, particularly ones with black oil sunflower seeds.

Interesting Fact: Carolina Chickadees have excellent recall. They can recall the position of thousands of concealed seeds, even beneath the snow, maintaining a steady food supply over the winter months.

Tips for Identification: The Carolina Chickadee is distinguished by its black head and bib, as well as its white cheeks. Their tiny size, lively demeanor, and high-pitched chick-a-dee-dee call all contribute to identification.

5. Mockingbird (Mimus polyglottos)

Description: This long-tailed songbird is a garden favorite. Adults have a grayish-brown coloration with a white belly and lengthy legs. They have large white wing bars and a black spot around the eye.

Habitat: Mockingbirds flourish in a wide range of environments, including backyards, gardens, forests, shrublands, and even urban settings. They easily adapt to human habitats and are recognized for their propensity to perch on exposed perches.

Interesting Fact: Mockingbirds are called for their exceptional ability to imitate other birds' songs as well as other noises in their surroundings. A single mockingbird can imitate the songs of hundreds of distinct species!

Identification tips: The Mockingbird has grayish-brown plumage, a long tail, white wing bars, and a black eye patch. Their tendency to perch conspicuously, as well as their various vocalizations, might provide useful hints.

Open Lands and Grasslands:

Beyond your home, South Texas' various landscapes provide a safe refuge for a variety of species that have adapted to these open settings. Let's look at some of the intriguing feathered creatures you could see in fields, meadows, and pastures.

6. Greater Roadrunner (Geococcyx californianus).

Description: This long-legged, ground-dwelling bird is easily identifiable. Adults have a rich brown coloration with a long, curved beak, a conspicuous crest on the head, and a long, blue-tipped tail that they keep erect when running.

Greater Roadrunner

- **Habitat:** ⌂ Greater Roadrunners inhabit dry scrublands, meadows, and open fields. They are especially well-suited to these open settings since their long legs allow for quick sprinting.
- **Interesting fact:** The Greater Roadrunner is the state bird of Texas. It is known as the "chaparral coyote" because of its speed and predatory habit. It eats insects, lizards, snakes, and small rodents.
- **Identification Tips:** The Greater Roadrunner is easily identified by its long legs, curved beak, large crest, and long tail. Their loud, piercing sounds also aid in their detection.

7. The Northern Mockingbird (Mimus polyglottos)

was previously described in Backyard Visitors.

While previously identified as a backyard visitor, the Northern Mockingbird may also be seen in wide fields and grasslands. Because of their adaptability to a variety of settings, they are a common and readily seen species in south Texas.

8. Killdeer (Charadrius vociferus)

- **Description:** This medium-sized shorebird often visits wide places such as fields, pastures, and even gravel parking lots. Adults have brown backs, white breasts, and bellies. They wear a striking black breast band and two black bands across their forehead.

Habitat: Killdeer live in a range of open settings, including meadows, fields, pastures, and even roofs in urban areas. They nest on the ground in a small scrape and use camouflage to hide.

Interesting Facts: Killdeer are famed for their elaborate injury-feigning displays, which they use to divert predators' attention away from their nests and babies. They will flap their wings and scream out loudly, directing the predator away from the fragile young.

Identification tips: The Killdeer's overall brown and white plumage, black breast band, and two black forehead bands are unmistakable. Their loud and piercing cries

9. Wild Turkey (Meleagris Gallopavo)

Wild Turkey

Description: This big, ground-dwelling bird is very stunning. Males (toms) stand out with their black body plumage, iridescent bronze breast feathers, and fleshy red wattle and snood dangling from their beaks. Females (hens) are significantly smaller and duller in color, having a brown body and barred feathers.

Habitat: Wild turkeys flourish in a wide range of settings, including woods, forests, farms, and even residential areas. They are superb runners who can use their camouflage to blend in with the environment.

Interesting Fact: Wild turkeys are endemic to North America and have had a profound impact on the continent's cultural heritage. They were previously an important food source for indigenous peoples and remain a popular game bird for hunters.

Tips for Identification: The male Wild Turkey's massive size and striking plumage make it easily identifiable. Females are often mistaken for other big birds, although their general brown appearance and banded feathers assist in identification. Listen to their loud gobbling noises, especially during the breeding season.

10. Cedar waxwings (Bombycilla cedrorum)

- **Description**: This lovely, medium-sized songbird has a distinct and graceful look. Adults have a brown back, a strong black mask, and a crest of feathers on their heads. They have noticeable waxy red ends on several of their secondary wing feathers. The underparts are light rufous, and the tail is tinged with yellow.

Cedar waxwings

Habitat: Cedar Waxwings live in a range of settings, including woods, forests, field borders, and even backyards in the winter. They are drawn to ripening trees and bushes and eat berries and other succulent fruits.

Interesting Fact: Cedar Waxwings display an odd habit known as "waxing," in which they devour massive amounts of fermented fruit, resulting in drunkenness. While the specific cause of this behavior is uncertain, it is thought to assist them in detoxifying from dangerous chemicals in the fruit or aid in digestion.

Tips for Identification: The Cedar Waxwing is distinguished by its brown back, black mask, crest, red waxy wing tips, and rufous underparts. They forage in flocks on fruiting trees and bushes.

Riparian Areas (River, Stream, Pond):

Riparian environments - rivers, streams, ponds, and their surrounding vegetation - are vital to many ecosystems and offer a safe refuge for a variety of species of aquatic birds. Let's look at some of the amazing feathered inhabitants that you could come across along South Texas's rivers.

11. Great Blue Heron (Ardea herodias)

Description: This big, long-legged wading bird is a breathtaking sight. Adults have a magnificent blue-gray coloration with a long, S-shaped neck, a bright yellow

beak, and lengthy legs. They have a conspicuous crest of feathers on their heads, which they may raise or decrease according to their mood.

Habitat:  Great Blue Herons live in various wetland settings, including rivers, streams, ponds, marshes, and coastal regions. They are patient stalkers who wade in shallow water, using their keen beaks to stab fish and other aquatic food.

Interesting fact: Great Blue Herons are friendly birds that typically breed in colonies known as heronries. These colonies may be extremely big, with hundreds of nesting pairs clustered in a single location.

Identification Tips: The Great Blue Heron is easily identified by its big size, long neck and legs, blue-gray plumage, and yellow beak. Look for them standing still in shallow water, ready to ambush prey.

12. Green Kingfisher (Chloroceryle americana)

Description: This colorful, medium-sized bird lives beside streams and in the woods. Adults are a stunning emerald green, with a huge, crested head and a long, pointed bill. They have white breasts and a blue ring across their chest.

Habitat: Green Kingfishers are found near rivers, streams, ponds, and canals, often perching on branches or wires that overlook the water. They are skilled hunters, plunging headfirst into the water to capture fish and tiny aquatic invertebrates.

Interesting Facts: Green Kingfishers, unlike other songbirds, make their nests by excavating burrows in clay banks. The male bird will construct a lengthy tunnel that ends in a chamber where the female will deposit her eggs.

Tips for Identification: The Green Kingfisher is distinguished by its brilliant green plumage, high-crested head, long beak, and the propensity to perch near bodies of water. Watch for their loud, rattling cries, sometimes known as "churring" or "rattling" sounds.

13. Yellow-billed Cuckoos (Coccyzus americanus)

Description: This slender, long-tailed bird spends the summer in South Texas. Adults have a grayish-brown coloration with a white abdomen and a long, yellow lower mandible. They feature a prominent black eye line and two white wing bars.

Habitat: Yellow-billed Cuckoos live in woods, forests, and riparian habitats with thick vegetation. Insectivores eat caterpillars, beetles, and other insects.

- **Interesting fact:** Yellow-billed Cuckoos are brood parasites. They deposit their eggs in the nests of other songbirds, such as cardinals and mockingbirds, and the unaware host parents rear the cuckoo baby as their own.
- **Identification tips:** The Yellow-billed Cuckoo may be identified by its thin body, long tail, grayish-brown plumage, white belly, and yellow lower mandible. Look for them sitting amid deep vegetation, often flicking their tails.

Lakes, Ponds, and Wetlands

Lakes, ponds, and wetlands are critical habitats that support aquatic life. These watery settings attract a varied range of species, including waterfowl, wading birds, and secretive rails. Here are two regular residents you'll meet.

14. Mallard duck (Anas platyrhynchos).

Description: This familiar dabbling duck is a widely distributed and plentiful species. The male Mallard stands out with its iridescent green head, brilliant yellow beak with a black tip (nail), and brown breast. The male drake has a white neck ring, a grayish-brown body, and black-and-white patterns on the wings.

The female (hen) is somewhat less striking, having mottled brown plumage and an orange beak with a black patch.

Mallard duck

- **Habitat:** Mallard Ducks live in a wide range of freshwater settings, including lakes, ponds, marshes, wetlands, and even urban parks with ponds. They are superb swimmers and dabblers, eating aquatic plants, seeds, and tiny invertebrates while tilting forward in the water.
- **Interesting fact:** Mallard ducks are one of the most prevalent waterfowl species worldwide. They have high sexual dimorphism, with males having vivid breeding plumage that attracts females.

- **Tips for Identification:** The male Mallard's distinctive green head and yellow beak make him simple to recognize. The female's mottled brown plumage is similar to other duck species, but its orange beak with a black patch distinguishes her. Look for them dipping in shallow water or swimming in lakes and ponds.

15. Northern Flickers (Colaptes auratus)

Description: This medium-sized woodpecker is often seen in forests, backyards, and even near telephone poles. Northern Flickers have a brown back with black bars, a white rump patch (visible while flying), and a white breast with black markings. They have a big, pointed beak and a strong tail that helps them climb trees.

An unusual trait is the presence of a yellow or red patch (depending on subspecies) beneath their wings, which is visible in flight.

Habitat: Northern Flickers may be found in a range of environments, including woods, forests, field margins, and even tree-lined backyards. They can cling to tree trunks and use their powerful beak to construct nesting chambers and retrieve insects from under the bark.

Interesting Fact: Unlike other woodpeckers, Northern Flickers often drum on metal surfaces such as gutters or flashing, giving them the moniker "yellowhammer."

Identification tips: The Northern Flicker's brown and black barred back, white rump, spotted breast, and long, pointed beak are distinctive. Look for a flash of yellow or red beneath their wings as they take flight. Their pounding sound might also be a useful indicator of their existence.

Brush and Woodland

Exploring the scrub and forests of South Texas reveals a world of intriguing bird variety. These thick ecosystems offer cover and food for a diverse range of species, including skulking thrashers, acrobatic woodpeckers, and stealthy wrens. Let's meet some of the regular inhabitants you can come across in this rich setting.

16.   Curve-billed   Thrasher (Toxostoma curvirostre).

Curve-billed Thrasher

Description: This big, long-tailed songbird hides in brushy thickets and forests. Adults have a deep brown coloration with a long, curved bill, a long tail, and a pronounced brow line over the eyes. They have a rufous patch on their wings that is apparent when flying.

Habitat: Curve-billed Thrashers inhabit dense thickets, brushy forests, hedgerows, and riparian environments. They are skilled at negotiating thick plants and spend a lot of time foraging on the ground for insects, fruits, and seeds.

- **Interesting Facts:** Curve-billed Thrashers are adept mimics, including a broad range of sounds in their songs, including other birds' cries, automobile alarms, and even human speech!
- **Identification tips:** The Curve-billed Thrasher's huge size, long tail, curved beak, and brown plumage are distinguishing features. Listen for their loud, intricate tunes, which often include copied noises. They are more likely to be heard than seen since they prefer to remain concealed in deep foliage.

17.   Golden-fronted   Woodpecker (Melanerpes aurifrons)

Description: This medium-sized woodpecker is often found in forests, densely forested neighborhoods, and riparian habitats. Adults have a black back with white patches, a red nape, and a brilliant yellow patch on the forehead (for males). They have a white belly with black stripes and a large, pointed beak.

Habitat: Golden-fronted woodpeckers may be found in a range of forested environments, including woods, forests, riparian regions, and well-established suburbs with mature trees. They forage actively, excavating holes for nests and extracting insects from under the bark.

Golden-fronted Woodpecker

Interesting Fact: Golden-fronted woodpeckers are cavity nesters, but unlike other woodpeckers, they may reuse previous cavities or even extend holes dug by other bird species.

Identification: The Golden-Fronted Woodpecker's black back with white dots, redneck, and brilliant yellow forehead (in males) are distinguishing traits. Listen for their drumming sound on trees and search for them clinging to trunks and branches while foraging for insects.

18. Carolina Wrens (Thryothorus ludovicianus)

Description: This little, lively songbird thrives in forests, thickets, and even densely vegetated backyards. Adults have a rich brown coloration with a long, rounded tail, a white belly, and a noticeable white forehead stripe. They have short, somewhat decurved bills.

Habitat: Carolina Wrens may be found in a wide range of forested environments, including woods, forests, thickets, field borders, and even well-vegetated backyards. They are very busy birds, fluttering through thick foliage looking for insects, spiders, and other invertebrates.

Interesting Fact: Carolina Wrens are cavity nesters that easily use nest boxes supplied in yards. They are territorial birds and will sing loudly to protect their area all year.

Identification tips: The Carolina Wren is distinguished by its tiny size, brown plumage, white eyebrow stripe, and long, rounded tail. Listen for their loud, complex melodies, which often include quick trills and whistles. Their habit of fluttering through thick foliage makes them difficult to see, but their melodies are instantly identifiable.

19. Plain Chachalaca (Ortalis vetula)

Description This big, long-legged bird is a distinctive dweller of thick thorn scrub and forests. Adults have a grayish-brown coloration with a long, black tail and an exposed red neck patch. Their heads are covered with a large feather crest, and their bills are strong and curved.

Habitat : Plain Chachalacas inhabit dense thickets, thorn scrub, forests, and riparian regions with brushy vegetation. They are terrestrial birds that spend most of their time foraging on the ground on fruits, seeds, and insects.

Interesting Fact: Plain Chachalacas are notable for their loud, boisterous vocalizations that resemble a chorus of "cha-cha-la-ca" cries. Individuals utilize these cries to communicate with one another and protect their area.

Identification tips: The Plain Chachalaca may be identified by its big size, long tail, grayish-brown plumage, exposed red neck patch, and crested head. Their loud, distinctive sounds are another significant indicator of their existence. However, since they favor deep cover, they might be difficult to see but easily heard.

20. White-winged Dove (Zenaida Asiatica)

Description: (formerly detailed in 4.1 Backyard Visitors): This gentle dove is a frequent South Texas inhabitant.

White-winged Dove

Adults are light grayish brown, with a long, pointed tail and a tiny head. They have a conspicuous black patch on each cheek and a white border along the trailing edge of their wings.

Habitat: 
White-winged Doves live in a range of open environments, including fields, meadows, backyards, and even brushy forests (especially in South Texas). They can easily adapt to urban and suburban surroundings.

Interesting Fact (previously mentioned in 4.1 Backyard Visitors): White-winged Doves communicate with one another via a melancholy cooing sound known as "who-cooks-for-you." Males and females both employ this vocalization.

Tips for Identification (as previously detailed in 4.1 Backyard Visitors): The White-winged Dove is distinguished by its general grayish-brown hue, long tail, and black cheek patch. Listen for their melancholy cooing cry to assist identification. White-winged Doves are generally found in open places, although they may sometimes be seen in brushy forests, notably in South Texas.

South Texas Specialty Birds.

South Texas's unusual position near the tip of North America allows birds with tropical affinities to visit the United States. This place is a paradise for birdwatchers looking for these unique inhabitants. Let's look at some of the birds you can come across that are unusual in other regions of the nation.

21. Green Jays (Cyanocorax yncas)

- **Description:** This bright jay thrives in forests, thorn scrub, and river environments. Adults are a stunning emerald green with a prominent blue crest, black markings around the eye and beak, and white wing bars. They have a long black tail and a thick, hooked beak.

Green Jays

Habitat: Green Jays live in a wide range of forested environments, including woods, thorn scrub, forests, and well-vegetated riparian regions. They are sociable birds that often travel in small groups to forage for insects, fruits, and nuts.

Interesting fact: Green Jays are clever birds recognized for their ability to utilize tools. They have been seen using sticks to pry open acorns and other foods.

Identification Tips: The Green Jay is easily identified by its striking green plumage, blue crest, black markings around the eye and beak, and white wing bars. Listen for their loud, noisy cries, which might sound like a combination of squawks, whistles, and chatter.

22. Altamira Orioles (Icterus gularis)

Description: This brightly colored oriole prefers forests, thorn scrub, and well-watered areas. The male Altamira Oriole stands out with its vivid orange head, breast, and back, black belly and wings, and white wing bar. The female is a duller yellow with black streaks on the breast and belly.

Habitat: Altamira Orioles live in a wide range of forested environments, including woods, thorn scrub, forests, riparian regions, and well-vegetated gardens and parks. They are insectivores and nectar feeders, consuming fruits, flowers, and insects.

Interesting Facts: Altamira Orioles are notable for their magnificent hanging nests made of plant fibers and strung from tree branches.

Tips for Identification: The male Altamira Oriole's vivid orange plumage with black and white markings is easily identifiable. The female is difficult, but her general golden hue and striped underparts set her apart from other orioles. Listen for their loud whistling tunes, which are often characterized as a sequence of clear, fluty notes.

23. Crested Caracara (Caracara cheriway).

Crested Caracara

Description: This rare falcon-like bird lives in meadows, pastures, and open brushlands. Adults are blackish-brown in color, with a large, yellow beak, a noticeable feather crest on the head, and long, yellow legs. Compared to real falcons, their tail is shorter and more rounded.

Habitat: Crested Caracaras inhabit open environments such as meadows, pastures, arable fields, and scattered forests. They are scavengers and opportunistic feeders who eat carrion, insects, small animals, and even fruits.

Interesting fact: Crested Caracaras are noted for their lively behavior and soaring flying patterns. They are often spotted perched on fence poles or flying in circles while looking for food.

Identification tips: The Crested Caracara's distinctive blackish-brown plumage, yellow beak, pronounced crest, long yellow legs, and short, rounded tail set it apart from other birds of prey. Look for them flying across broad spaces or perched on conspicuous vantage points.

24. Buff-bellied Hummingbird (Amazilia yucatanensis)

Description: This hummingbird is one of the biggest in the United States. Males have an iridescent green neck and breast, as well as a characteristic buff patch on their belly (thus the name). Their back is bronzy brown, and they have a long, red beak. Females are similar in appearance, but lack an iridescent throat and have a duller overall hue.

Habitat: Buff-bellied Hummingbirds enjoy dense thickets, brushy forests, thorn scrub, and riparian regions rich in blooming plants. They are drawn to hummingbird feeders, especially in the northern regions of their territory when winters are harsher.

Interesting fact: Buff-bellied Hummingbirds are partly migratory. Populations in the north of their range move south during the winter, but southern populations may stay year-round.

Tips for Identification: The Buff-bellied Hummingbird's bigger size (for a hummingbird), iridescent green neck (males), buff belly, and red bill aid in identification. Look for them hovering near floral plants or feeders, and listen for the high-pitched buzz of their wings.

25. Scissor-tailed Flycatcher (Tyrannus forficatus).

Description: This distinctive flycatcher thrives in open environments such as meadows, pastures, and agricultural fields. Adults are grayish-brown in color with a white belly and a long, highly forked tail that resembles a pair of scissors (diagnostic characteristic). They have a black mask over their eyes and a white patch on the outside margins of their tail.

Scissor-tailed Flycatcher

Habitat: Scissor-tailed Flycatchers inhabit open environments such as meadows, pastures, agricultural fields, scattered trees, and forest borders. They are agile insectivores who grab flying insects in mid-air using acrobatic moves.

Interesting Fact: The Scissor-tailed Flycatcher has the longest tail in proportion to the body size of any North American bird. The tail may get up to twice as long as the body!

Identification Tips: The Scissor-tailed Flycatcher is easily identified by its long, highly forked tail. Their grayish-brown plumage, white belly, and black mask around the eye make identification easier. Look for them poised on fence posts, wires, or trees, waiting for flying insects.

Beyond Your Backyard: Birding Hot Spots in South Texas

South Texas, with its various landscapes and strategic position near the tip of North America, provides a home for both resident and migratory birds. This chapter will take you outside your home to some of the region's best birding locations. Each site has a distinct collection of avian inhabitants, ensuring an exciting bird watching experience. So grab your binoculars, dust out your field guide, and prepare to visit South Texas' amazing birding hotspots!

State Parks:

Bentsen-Rio Grande Valley State Park (Mission): This park preserves approximately 680 acres of Rio Grande floodplain habitat, providing a home for riparian and brush birds. The park has several birding routes, including the famed Resaca Trail, which weaves through dense thickets and resacas (oxbow lakes), providing an ideal habitat for songbirds, warblers, and migratory ducks. Look for Curve-billed Thrashers, Green Jays, Altamira Orioles, and even the rare Long-tailed Dickcissel in the grasslands. The park also has a hawk-watching platform overlooking the Rio Grande, which is an excellent place to look for raptors such as Harris's Hawks, Common Black Hawks, and Zone-tailed Hawks flying on thermals.

Laguna Atascosa State Park (Zapata): With approximately 88,000 acres of different ecosystems, Laguna Atascosa is a birders' paradise. The park is a mix of forests, thorn scrub, freshwater resacas, and tidal flats that attract an incredible variety of wildlife. Golden-fronted Woodpeckers, Plain Chachalacas, and Buff-breasted Flycatchers are among the nesting species seen along the Chaparral Trail. Explore the Long Loop Drive for a chance to see rare species like Tamaulipas Crows, Aplomado Falcons, and even the endangered Least Grebe in bigger resacas. The park also provides a good opportunity for wading birding, with Roseate Spoonbills, Green Herons, and Common Yellowthroats frequenting the shallow ponds and marshy regions.

Aransas National Wildlife Refuge (Austwell): While best known for its wintering whooping crane population, Aransas National Wildlife Refuge provides excellent birding opportunities all year. The refuge has a diverse range of habitats, including coastal prairies, tidal flats, marshes, and forests. The Matanzas Bird Blind is a must-see for birders, with a strategic observation platform overlooking a series of ponds and grasslands. You may view a variety of waterfowl, shorebirds, and wading birds here, including Mottled Ducks, American Avocets, and Willet. The Woodland Trail of the refuge also provides great birding opportunities, with resident specialties such as Gray Jays, Eastern Bluebirds, and Great Crested Flycatchers.

Wildlife Refuges:

Santa Ana National Wildlife Refuge (Allamo): This 2,000-acre refuge preserves a critical tract of Lower Rio Grande Valley habitat. The flowing Rio Grande and its riparian woodland give excellent birdwatching chances. The Frontera Trail is an excellent starting place, providing stunning views of the river and attracting a diverse range of resident and migratory species. Keep an eye out for flycatchers such as Tropical Kingbirds and Streaked Flycatchers darting among the trees. Long-billed Rails and

Virginia Warblers may live in the thick understory. The Alto Vista Unit, accessible via boat across the Rio Grande, provides a unique viewpoint and opportunities to witness Ringed Rails and Buff-collared Orioles.

Lower Rio Grande Valley National Wildlife Refuge (many locations): This vast refuge spans over 100,000 acres over four distinct units: Santa Ana, Buras Cienegas, Las Palomas, and Resaca de la Palma. The refuge's various habitats, which range from thick thorn scrub to freshwater resacas and coastal plains, offer a banquet for both resident and migrant birds. The small ponds of the Buras Cienegas Unit attract a variety of waterbirds, including Roseate Spoonbills, Least Grebes, and Northern Shovelers. The Resaca de la Palma Unit has outstanding riparian birding chances, including Green Kingfishers, Altamira Orioles, and the uncommon Stillman's Willow Flycatcher. Birding along the levee pathways throughout the refuge may be rewarding, with the possibility of seeing raptors such as Common Ravens and Caracaras hunting for prey.

Salinity Trap (Port Isabel): This one-of-a-kind birding hotspot is a former wastewater treatment plant that has been converted into a shorebird sanctuary. During their travels, shorebirds rely on shallow ponds and mudflats as stopover habitats. During peak season (spring and autumn), the exposed mudflats are teeming with a diverse range of shorebirds in different breeding plumages. Look for colorful migrants such as Ruddy Turnstones, Sanderlings, and Semipalmated Plovers, as well as resident species like Killdeer and Long-billed Curlew. The neighboring observation platform provides a close-up view of these amazing birds without disturbing them. Wading birds, including Great Egrets and White-faced Ibises, feed in the shallow ponds.

Birding Trails:

The World Birding Center (many locations) is a one-of-a-kind network of nine birding sites that spans a 120-mile length of the Rio Grande Valley from South Padre Island to Roma. Each location has a unique ecosystem and its own avian specialty. Explore the Edinburg Scenic Wetlands to witness wading birds like Roseate Spoonbills and Limpkins, while the Quinta Mazatlan World Birding Center near McAllen has a lovely botanical garden with resident specialties like Olive

Sparrows and Altamira Orioles. The Santa Ana Hawkwatching Area is an excellent place to observe migratory raptors flying on thermals, while the Falcon Dam overlooks the Rio Grande and gives opportunities to see uncommon riparian species such as Zone-tailed Hawks and Kingfishers.

Great Texas Coastal Birding Trail: This large trail network spans over 600 miles of shoreline and contains several birding hotspots throughout the Texas Gulf Coast. The Lower Texas Coast region, which stretches from Baffin Bay to Brownsville, is a birders' paradise. Mustang Island State Park is well-known for its diverse shorebird and wading bird populations. Visit the South Padre Island World Birding Center, which provides good prospects for coastal birding, with the possibility of seeing terns, gulls, and jaegers offshore. The Laguna Atascosa NWR Visitor Center offers picturesque views and pathways that weave through deep thorn scrub, ideal for seeing secretive species like Tamaulipas Crows and Aplomado Falcons.

Research the birding hotspots: Before leaving, spend some time researching the particular birding places you want to visit. This will allow you to better understand the ecosystems, target species, and suggested pathways for each area. Many birding websites and apps provide current information on bird sightings and birding areas.

Choose the appropriate time of day: Birds are most active in the early morning and late afternoon. Plan your birding trips around these times to increase your chances of seeing and hearing birds.

Dress Appropriately: Choose comfortable clothes and footwear suited for the terrain you'll be exploring. Long trousers, sturdy shoes, and a cap are crucial for protecting oneself from the weather and thorny bushes.

Bring Necessary Birding Equipment: Purchase a decent pair of binoculars with at least 8x magnification for clear views of distant birds. A field guide unique to the area can help you identify the birds you see. If you own a spotting scope, consider bringing it for more comprehensive observations.

Be Patient and Observant: Birding requires a strong eye for detail. Listen for bird songs and cries, and keep an eye out for movement in the trees, shrubs, and open spaces. Minimize disturbance: Always stick to authorized pathways and avoid making loud sounds that may startle the birds. Be aware of your surroundings and avoid approaching nests or nesting sites.

Keep a Birding Journal: Write down your birding encounters in a journal. Make a note of the date, location, species, and any unusual behaviors you noticed. This might be a useful tool for monitoring your progress and recalling your bird-watching excursions.

Following these suggestions and experiencing South Texas' outstanding birding locations will put you on the path to becoming a birding enthusiast and appreciating the beauties of the avian world. Remember that birding is an ongoing learning process, full of fresh discoveries and chances to interact with nature. So, take your binoculars, visit the trails, and prepare to be astounded by South Texas' vast and intriguing bird population!

Birding Throughout the Year—A Seasonal Guide to South Texas' Avian Spectacle

South Texas, with its subtropical temperature and diversified habitats, is home to a thriving bird community all year. Understanding these seasonal differences is essential for increasing your birding success in the area. This chapter digs into the intriguing world of South Texas' resident and migratory birds, emphasizing the distinct spectacles that each season brings.

Spring (March to May):

Spring is a dynamic season in South Texas, with blooming wildflowers, returning migrants, and an increase in mating activity. Bird melodies fill the air as resident species such as Curve-billed Thrashers, Golden-fronted Woodpeckers, and Carolina Wrens establish territories and nests.

Migratory Influx: Spring ushers in a rush of colorful migratory migrants fleeing severe winter conditions further north. Warblers, the gems of the bird world, become a common sight. Look for vividly colorful birds such as the Black-throated Green Warbler, Yellow Warbler, and magnificent Painted Bunting darting around the trees and shrubbery. Flycatchers such as the Eastern Kingbird and Great Kiskadee join the chorus, adding to its dynamic energy.

Wader show: Spring is an excellent time to see the magnificent show of shorebird migration. Coastal regions such as South Padre Island and the Lower Rio Grande Valley become popular stopovers for these long-distance tourists. Shorebirds of varied breeding plumages, embellished with vivid colors and elaborate patterns, populate the mudflats and small lakes. Look for fascinating species like the Ruddy Turnstone, Semipalmated Sandpiper, and Willet feeding and resting before continuing their northward migration.

Raptor Rendezvous: During the spring, raptors flying on thermals travel north. Look for Broad-winged Hawks, Swainson's Hawks, and the spectacular Mississippi Kite circling above. The Santa Ana Hawkwatching Area in the Lower Rio Grande Valley is an excellent site to see this spectacular aerial spectacle.

Summer (June to August):

Summer in South Texas brings scorching heat, but birdwatching chances abound. Resident birds are busy raising their young, with fledglings emerging from nests and exploring the world for the first time. Summer nights are ideal for hearing the distinctive sounds of young birds asking for food from their parents.

The breeding season is in full swing, with resident birds focusing on rearing their broods. Observe the exquisite nest-building talents of Altamira Orioles and Buff-breasted Flycatchers. Keep a lookout for colorful fledglings perched precariously on trees, imitating their parents' cries and learning to scavenge for food.

Bush Area Specialties: The summer months are ideal for exploring South Texas' bush area in quest of local specialties. The deep thickets and thorn scrub offer habitat for secretive species such as Plain Chachalacas, Tamaulipas Crows (Laguna Atascosa NWR), and Long-billed Rails (Santa Ana). Patience and careful attention are required to detect these elusive birds.

Shorebird Shore Up: In late summer, shorebirds migrate southward from their nesting sites in the Arctic. Similar to spring, coastal regions are teeming with shorebirds in different molting plumages, moving from breeding colors to more muted winter garb. This is an excellent chance to study shorebirds in huge numbers and improve your identification abilities.

Fall (September to November):

Fall provides a pleasant break from the summer heat and ushers in another stunning migratory season. Avian variety expands as southern migrants join the local species, resulting in a colorful birding display.

Fall Migration Frenzy: Fall is the best time to see the incredible phenomena of bird migration. A large number of warblers, buntings, flycatchers, and orioles migrate to

South Texas, altering the landscape with their colorful plumage and bright melodies. Birding hotspots around the shore and riparian corridors are buzzing with activity, allowing birders to observe a diverse range of species in a single visit.

Raptor Bonanza: Fall is an excellent season to view raptors in South Texas. Predatory birds such as Broad-winged Hawks, Swainson's Hawks, and Mississippi Kites move south in great numbers, typically flying in kettles (spiraling groups) to take advantage of thermal updrafts. The Lower Rio Grande Valley's strategic position makes it an ideal place to view this amazing show of bird acrobatics.

Hummingbird Highway: South Texas is an important layover location for migratory hummingbirds. Look for the spectacular Buff-bellied Hummingbird, one of the biggest hummingbird species in the United States, feasting on blossoming flowers and hummingbird feeders. During peak migration seasons, other hummingbird species, such as the Ruby-throated Hummingbird and the Rufous Hummingbird, may be seen fluttering between flowers, adding to the colorful spectacle.

Winter offers a feeling of calm to the South Texas birding landscape. Many migratory birds have left for warmer climates, but resident species continue to thrive, and some winter visitors come, adding to the avifauna's diversity.

Winter Residents: While overall bird variety decreases significantly in the winter, resident species such as Curve-billed Thrashers, Golden-fronted Woodpeckers, and Carolina Wrens stay active all season. These birds have adapted to lower temperatures and shorter days by foraging and defending their territory.

Waterfowl Wonderland: During the winter, South Texas' coastal regions and freshwater marshes become wintering habitats for waterfowl. Look for ducks such as Mottled Ducks, Northern Shovelers, and Gadwalls on the ponds and marshes. Geese such as Greater White-fronted and Snow Geese may also be seen in agricultural fields or resting on sandbars near the Rio Grande. Winter is an excellent time to get out of your spotting scope and admire the beauty of these amazing birds.

Lingering delicacies: Keep a look out for several winter delicacies that may still be available in South Texas. These include raptors such as the Zone-tailed Hawk, which likes the Rio Grande Valley's riparian corridors, as well as the endangered Aplomado Falcon wintering population in the region's south (Laguna Atascosa NWR).

Conclusion:

All year, South Texas is a birder's paradise. With its diversified ecosystems, strategic position, and resident and migratory birds, the area offers several opportunities to see and enjoy the beauties of the avian world. Understanding seasonal differences and organizing your birding outings appropriately can improve your overall birding experience. So, grab your binoculars, pick a season, and go off to experience South Texas' magnificent birds!

Cultivating Your Birding Legacy—The Enduring Value of a Birding Journal

Birdwatching is a rewarding hobby that links us to the natural world and cultivates a profound respect for bird biodiversity. Beyond the first joy of discovering a new species, maintaining a birding notebook transforms this interest into a gratifying lifetime endeavor. This chapter discusses the multiple advantages of keeping a birdwatching notebook and offers helpful hints for documenting your observations thoroughly and interestingly.

The Enduring Value of a Birding Journal:

Enhanced Learning and Memory: Recording your bird observations forces you to pay more attention to details, enhancing your identification abilities and cementing your understanding of bird behavior, habitat preferences, and vocalizations. Referencing your journal entries over time helps you monitor your birding progress, assess your learning curve, and reflect on previous birding excursions.

Personalized Field Guide: Over time, your birding notebook will evolve into a personalized field guide based on your individual birding experiences. Detailed notes on bird sightings in different locales, coupled with pictures or drawings (if included), maybe a useful reference for future expeditions. Imagine flicking through your diary and seeing comprehensive notes and illustrations of that elusive bird you observed years ago, which would help you identify it in future encounters.

A Chronicle of Avian Activity: Your birding notebook becomes a record of avian activity in your local area or the locations you visit. By attentively noting species occurrences throughout the year, you provide essential data for long-term citizen science programs. This aggregate knowledge is critical for monitoring bird populations, following migratory patterns, and evaluating the health of ecosystems.

Sharing the Joy of Birds: Your birding notebook may be a great way to share your enthusiasm for birds with others. Detailed descriptions, drawings, and pictures might pique the attention of other birders or instill a passion for birds in future generations.

Consider the thrill of a kid browsing through your diary and seeing vivid artwork or insightful comments about the birds you've seen.

Tips for Documenting Sightings in Your Birding Journal

Essential Details: Each notebook post should provide basic information about your birding experience. Keep a record of your birding trip's date, time, and location. Identify the precise birding hotspot or location you visited. Take note of the meteorological conditions, since these might impact bird behavior.

Species List: Make a complete list of all the bird species you see throughout your expedition. Make a note of how many members of each species you see. This information might be useful for assessing seasonal patterns or the habitat preferences of certain bird species.

Detailed observations: Go beyond just listing the birds you observed. Make thorough notes on their behavior. Were they singing in the trees, feeding on the ground, or sitting on branches? Have you seen any fascinating interactions between various species? Recording this information will improve your birding experience and give significant insights into avian behavior.

Habitat Notes: Describe the environment in which you met the birds. Were you birding in a deep forest, a verdant riparian corridor, or a coastal salt marsh? Noting the habitat type helps you understand the ecological requirements of various bird species and allows for more focused birdwatching in the future.

Sketches and pictures (Optional): Although not required, incorporating sketches or pictures of the species you see will greatly improve your birding notebook. If you're artistically inclined, do brief field drawings to capture the essential physical characteristics of the birds you witnessed. Photographs, if obtainable, may be very useful for identification.

Document Rarities: If you come across a rare bird or species that lives outside of its normal range, take detailed notes. Include extensive notes about its physical characteristics, behavior, and the environment in which you witnessed it. Consider drawing the bird or taking a picture (if ethical) to supplement your documentation. Sharing these findings with local birding groups or internet forums might benefit the birding community.

Keeping a birding notebook is a gratifying activity that promotes a stronger connection to the avian world. By following these guidelines and diligently noting your observations, you will create a valuable resource that will enhance your birding experience for years to come.

Birding with Responsibility: Ethics, Conservation, and Coexistence.

Birdwatching is really about celebrating nature and the great variety of bird life. Ethical birding habits are critical for providing a good experience for both birds and birders while reducing human influence on these interesting species. This chapter highlights the significance of birding ethics and discusses how you might help bird conservation efforts.

The Birder's Code of Ethics:

- **Respect wildlife:** Birds are wild animals with inherent rights that require our respect. Don't approach nests or disrupt breeding colonies. Loud sounds or rapid movements may startle birds and disturb their normal routines. Keep a safe distance and use binoculars or spotting scopes to get a closer look.

- **Minimize Your Impact:** Strive to be a conscientious environmental steward. Stay on approved routes to prevent trampling plants and reduce ecological damage. Please dispose of any rubbish appropriately and leave no evidence of your presence. Be aware of your surroundings and refrain from introducing invasive plant species that may disturb the ecology.

- **Reduce Playback:** The excessive use of recorded bird sounds and songs to attract birds is a contentious issue. It may alter normal avian behavior and impair their capacity to communicate properly. Use your birding abilities and understanding of bird cries to find birds naturally. If you decide to utilize playback selectively and ethically, make sure you understand the possible negative consequences and only use it when required for identification.

- **Sharing is Caring:** The birding community values teamwork and the appropriate exchange of knowledge. Document your observations in detail in your birding diary, and consider reporting them to online birding platforms or local birding groups. This information helps to important citizen science efforts that monitor bird numbers and migratory patterns. However, do not publicize the locations of critical nesting sites or unusual bird observations, particularly online. This may increase birding traffic and perhaps kill birds.

Supporting Bird Conservation:

Bird populations suffer a variety of threats, including habitat loss, climate change, and illegal hunting. Fortunately, you can take meaningful measures to help bird conservation efforts:

Support Conservation Organizations: Join or give to respected bird conservation organizations such as the National Audubon Society, Cornell Lab of Ornithology, or local birding groups. These organizations play an important role in bird conservation by protecting habitat, educating people, and conducting research.

Volunteer Your Time: Many conservation groups depend on devoted volunteers to achieve their objectives. Consider volunteering for habitat restoration initiatives, bird population surveys, or educational outreach activities. Contributing your talents and time immediately aids bird conservation initiatives.

- **Advocate for Bird-Friendly Practices:** Protect birds and their habitats. Encourage local governments to undertake bird-friendly initiatives in your area, such as planting native plants, decreasing pesticide usage, and establishing wildlife corridors. You may also support companies that encourage environmentally friendly practices and avoid goods that contribute to habitat destruction.

- **Make Informed Consumer Decisions:** Bird-friendly choices extend to your daily routine. When buying coffee or wood goods, search for certificates that guarantee sustainable practices and limit deforestation, which may harm bird habitats. Making smart purchase choices may send a strong statement while also supporting firms that are dedicated to environmental sustainability.

- Birding with conscience instills a feeling of responsibility for the avian world. By practicing ethical birdwatching and actively supporting conservation initiatives, you may become a bird steward and help to ensure that these amazing species will survive in the future.

Appendix A: Glossary of 25 Birding Terms

1. **Binoculars (Binoculars):** A handheld optical device with two telescopes aligned side-by-side, used for magnifying distant objects, essential for birding.
2. **Bird feeder:** A structure designed to provide food for birds, often placed in backyards or gardens to attract birds for observation.
3. **Birding:** The activity of observing and identifying birds in their natural habitat.
4. **Bogey Bird:** A bird species that a birder has repeatedly failed to identify successfully.
5. **Chick:** A young bird that has hatched from an egg but is not yet fully grown.
6. **Dipping:** Missing the opportunity to see a particular bird species, often after traveling a significant distance.
7. **Fledgling:** A young bird that has recently left the nest and is learning to fly and forage for food on its own.

8. **Hawkwatching:** The focused observation of raptors (birds of prey) such as hawks, eagles, and falcons, often from a designated location.

9. **Habitat:** The natural environment in which a particular plant or animal species lives.

10. **LBJ (Little Brown Job):** A humorous term used for a small, brown bird that a birder is unable to identify due to its lack of distinctive markings.

11. **Life Bird (Lifer):** A bird species that a birder observes for the first time in their life, a significant achievement for birders.

12. **Migration:** The seasonal movement of birds from one breeding ground to another.

13. **Nest:** A structure built by a bird to lay and incubate its eggs and raise its young.

14. **Patch:** A local area frequented by birders due to its reliability in attracting a particular bird species or diverse assemblage of birds.

15. **Pelagic Birding:** Birding from a boat at sea, targeting seabirds, albatrosses, petrels, and other oceanic bird species.

16. **Raptor:** A bird of prey with sharp talons and a hooked beak, such as a hawk, eagle, or owl.

17. **Riparian:** Relating to or located on the bank of a river or stream.

18. **Shorebird:** A bird that frequents the edges of oceans, lakes, or rivers, often with long legs and a bill adapted for feeding in shallow water.

19. **Spotting Scope:** A high-powered, monocular telescope used for detailed observation of distant birds.

20. **Territorial:** Behaving in a way that defends a particular area (territory) from other individuals of the same species.
21. **Twitching:** Traveling a long distance specifically to see a rare bird species.
22. **Warbler:** A small, insectivorous songbird, often brightly colored, belonging to the wood warbler family.
23. **Wading Bird:** A long-legged bird that frequents shallow water to feed on fish, insects, and other aquatic prey, such as a heron, egret, or flamingo.
24. **Waterfowl:** A group of aquatic birds, including ducks, geese, swans, and loons.
25. **Winter plumage:** The distinctive feathers and coloration of a bird species during the winter season, often duller or more cryptic compared to its breeding plumage.

Appendix B: Resources for South Texas Birders

Birdwatching Clubs:

- Lower Rio Grande Valley Bird Club (LRGVBC): https://www.facebook.com/groups/RGVbirding/
- Corpus Christi Bird Club (CCBC): https://www.facebook.com/CBCBirdClub/
- San Antonio Audubon Society (SAAS): https://www.saaudubon.org/
- Texas Ornithological Society (TOS): https://www.texasbirds.org/

Nature Centers:

- World Birding Center (multiple locations): https://www.valleynaturecenter.org/about-vnc
- Santa Ana National Wildlife Refuge Visitor Center (Allamo): https://www.fws.gov/refuge/santa-ana
- Laguna Atascosa National Wildlife Refuge Visitor Center (Zapata): https://www.fws.gov/refuge/laguna-atascosa
- South Padre Island World Birding Center (South Padre Island): https://www.spibirding.com/

Online Resources:

- eBird (citizen science platform for bird observations): https://ebird.org/home
- Texas Parks & Wildlife Department - Birding in Texas: https://tpwd.texas.gov/education/resources/texas-junior-naturalists/watching-wildlife/texas-birds
- The Cornell Lab of Ornithology - All About Birds: https://www.allaboutbirds.org/news/
- National Audubon Society: https://www.audubon.org/

Additional Resources:

- Birding apps: Merlin Bird ID, Audubon Bird Guide, Sibley Birds
- Field guides: The Birds of Texas by Peterson Field Guides, Kaufman Field Guide to Birds of North America

Note: This is not an exhaustive list, and there are many other birding clubs, nature centers, and online resources available in South Texas. Conduct online searches to find resources specific to your area of interest.

Appendix C: Index of Birds (South Texas)

This index includes birds mentioned throughout the guide and some additional species commonly found in South Texas.

A

- Altamira Oriole
- Aplomado Falcon (endangered)
- Buff-breasted Flycatcher
- Buff-bellied Hummingbird

B

- Black-bellied Whistling Duck
- Black-capped Vireo
- Blue Jay
- Blue-winged Teal
- Broad-winged Hawk

C

- Cattle Egret
- Common Grackle
- Curve-billed Thrasher

D

- Dickcissel

E

- Eastern Kestrel
- Eastern Phoebe
- Eastern Screech-Owl

G

- Golden-fronted Woodpecker
- Greater White-fronted Goose
- Green Jay

H

- Harris's Hawk
- Horned Lark

I

- Inca Dove

K

- Killdeer
- Kingfisher (unspecified) - Consider listing specific species like Ringed Kingfisher
- Kingfisher (Belted Kingfisher) - Add if present in your area
- Ladder-backed Woodpecker

- Loggerhead Shrike
- Long-billed Curlew

M

- Mottled Duck

N

- Northern Cardinal
- Northern Flicker
- Northern Harrier
- Northern Mockingbird
- Northern Shoveler

P

- Plain Chachalaca

R

- Red-headed Woodpecker
- Red-shouldered Hawk (common in most of Texas, but presence in South Texas needs confirmation)
- Red-tailed Hawk
- Ringed Kingfisher (if present in your area)
- Roadrunner
- Ruby-crowned Kinglet
- Ruddy Turnstone
- Rufous Hummingbird (winter visitor)

S

- Sanderling
- Savannah Sparrow
- Semipalmated Sandpiper
- Snow Goose
- Song Sparrow (winter visitor in some areas)
- Swainson's Hawk

T

- Tamaulipas Crow
- Tree Swallow (winter visitor in some areas)

W

- White-collared Seedeater
- White-faced Ibis
- Willet

Note: This list is not exhaustive. The incredible diversity of South Texas avifauna includes hundreds of bird species. Refer to field guides and online resources for a more comprehensive listing.

www.ingramcontent.com/pod-product-compliance
Lightning Source LLC
Chambersburg PA
CBHW050805250726
48653CB00006B/2089